Penguins

Carey Molter

Published by SandCastle™, an imprint of ABDO Publishing Company, 4940 Viking Drive, Edina, Minnesota 55435.

Printed in the United States.

Cover and interior photo credits: Corbis Images, Corel, PhotoDisc

Library of Congress Cataloging-in-Publication Data

Molter, Carey, 1973-
    Penguins / Carey Molter.
       p. cm. -- (Zoo animals)
    ISBN 1-57765-562-1
    1. Penguins--Juvenile literature. [1. Penguins.] I. Title

    QL696.S473 M66 2001
    598.47--dc21

                                                    2001022009

The SandCastle concept, content, and reading method have been reviewed and approved by a national advisory board including literacy specialists, librarians, elementary school teachers, early childhood education professionals, and parents.

Let Us Know

After reading the book, SandCastle would like you to tell us your stories about reading. What is your favorite page? Was there something hard that you needed help with? Share the ups and downs of learning to read. We want to hear from you! To get posted on the Abdo Publishing Company Web site, send us email at:

sandcastle@abdopub.com

About SandCastle™

Nonfiction books for the beginning reader

- Basic concepts of phonics are incorporated with integrated language methods of reading instruction. Most words are short, and phrases, letter sounds, and word sounds are repeated.

- Readability is determined by the number of words in each sentence, the number of characters in each word, and word lists based on curriculum frameworks.

- Full-color photography reinforces word meanings and concepts.

- "Words I Can Read" list at the end of each book teaches basic elements of grammar, helps the reader recognize the words in the text, and builds vocabulary.

- Reading levels are indicated by the number of flags on the castle.

Note: Some pages in this book contain more than five words in order to more clearly convey the concept of the book.

Look for more SandCastle books in these three reading levels:

Level 1 (one flag)	**Level 2** (two flags)	**Level 3** (three flags)

Grades Pre-K to K 5 or fewer words per page	**Grades K to 1** 5 to 10 words per page	**Grades 1 to 2** 10 to 15 words per page

Penguins **are birds.**

Some penguins live in zoos.

Many penguins live in cold places.

Penguins **lay eggs.**

Penguins **cannot fly.**

Penguins **swim well.**

Penguins **have webbed feet.**

Baby penguins are
called chicks.

Have you seen a penguin?

Words I Can Read

Nouns

A noun is a person, place, or thing

birds (BURDZ) p. 5
chicks (CHIKSS) p. 19
eggs (EGZ) p. 11
feet (FEET) p. 17
penguin (PEN-gwin) p. 21
penguins (PEN-gwinz)
pp. 5, 7, 9, 11, 13, 15, 17, 19
places (PLAYSS-iz) p. 9
zoos (ZOOZ) p. 7

22

Verbs

A verb is an action or being word

are (AR) pp. 5, 19
called (KAWLD) p. 19
cannot (KAN-ot) p. 13
fly (FLYE) p. 13
have (HAV) pp. 17, 21
lay (LAY) p. 11
live (LIV) pp. 7, 9
seen (SEEN) p. 21
swim (SWIM) p. 15

More About Penguins
Match the Words to the Pictures

chick

webbed feet

eggs

fly

24